Timothy Joins Paul

Acts 16:1–5, 2 Timothy 1:1–7, 2 Timothy 4:14–17;
and 1 Timothy 1:3 for children

Written by Erik Rottmann
Illustrated by Joel Snyder

CONCORDIA PUBLISHING HOUSE · SAINT LOUIS

One day in Ephesus, a scroll
Arrived from far away.
It came for Pastor Timothy.
It brightened up his day.

As Timothy read through the scroll
That he had just received,
He thought about his childhood days,
To when he first believed.

He thought about two lovely saints
Who taught him all they knew
About the Scriptures of the Lord.
The words they spoke were true.

His grandma was named Lois,
She loved to teach God's Word.
Together with his mother, Eunice,
He learned of Christ, the Lord.

The Living Word these ladies spoke
Performed a mighty deed:
The Holy Spirit gave him faith,
Which grew up, like a seed.

The faith that grew in Timothy
Gave him a love for all.
He served the Lord in his hometown,
Until he met Saint Paul.

Paul traveled throughout many lands.
The Lord sent him to preach,
To baptize people in God's name
And with His Word, to teach.

Paul asked if Timothy would come
And help him preach the Word;
To tell about the risen Lord
To those who had not heard.

Together Paul and Timothy
Both traveled sea and earth
And through the mighty Word they preached
The Spirit gave new birth.

The gift of faith is this new birth,
Implanted like a seed
Within the hearts of those who heard
So that they could believe.

The newly planted churches grew
Like gardens for the Lord.
It wasn't Paul or Timothy!
God's grace had been outpoured.

But now these two friends were apart,
Each in a different place.
And that's why Paul had sent the scroll
To strengthen his friend's faith.

When Timothy rolled up the scroll
He wore a thankful smile,
Remembering how their dear Lord
Protected them each mile.

For even though they traveled far
And sometimes went to jail,
God's Spirit had done mighty things;
His living Word prevailed.

The news of Jesus' death and life
Is still proclaimed today.
And through this Word, the Spirit works
In a mighty way.

The gift of faith God gives to you
Will grow just like a seed,
Producing fruit like love and hope
Expressed through word and deed.

Dear Parents,

"The Word of God . . . is at work in you who believe" (1 Thessalonians 2:13). This book illustrates how God's Word worked powerfully in Timothy, Paul's companion. Through the Word, God the Holy Spirit not only planted faith in Timothy, but He also caused that faith to thrive and produce fruit, commonly called "good works." Working through Timothy, God called many more people to faith as well, "so the churches were strengthened in the faith and grew daily in numbers" (Acts 16:5).

After reading this story, discuss with your child the sorts of good works that result from God's gift of faith. These include not only "great" deeds, like Timothy's preaching to the world, but they also include the works common to every Christian: obedience to parents and authorities, faithful attendance at worship, pious living, and the like. With your child, pray that God would continue His work in you, building you up in faith and trust in the Lord Jesus Christ and emboldening you to speak God's life-giving Word to others. Pray that they, too, may become "a planting of the Lord for the display of His splendor" (Isaiah 61:3).

The Author